CHARLES MCMULLEN

Alife
in
Bits

the memoirs of a cheerful bipolar

To All the
Eastleigh folk.
Enjoy My Story

Charles McMullen

CHARLES MCMULLEN

A life
in
Bits

the memoirs of a cheerful bipolar

MEREO
Cirencester

Mereo Books

1A The Wool Market Dyer Street Cirencester Gloucestershire GL7 2PR
An imprint of Memoirs Publishing www.mereobooks.com

A Life In Bits: 978-1-86151-139-3

First published in Great Britain in 2014
by Mereo Books, an imprint of Memoirs Publishing

Copyright ©2014

The address for Memoirs Publishing Group Limited can be found at
www.memoirspublishing.com

The Memoirs Publishing Group Ltd Reg. No. 7834348

The Memoirs Publishing Group supports both The Forest Stewardship Council® (FSC®) and the PEFC® leading international forest-certification organisations. Our books carrying both the FSC label and the PEFC® and are printed on FSC®-certified paper. FSC® is the only forest-certification scheme supported by the leading environmental organisations including Greenpeace. Our paper procurement policy can be found at
www.memoirspublishing.com/environment

Cover design - Ray Lipscombe

Typeset in 12/18pt Plantin
by Wiltshire Associates Publisher Services Ltd. Printed and bound in Great Britain by Printondemand-Worldwide, Peterborough PE2 6XD

Foreword

From the River Itchen's waters and the forest green Hampshire parks to the sunny sea and the seaside of the south coast.

From the busy, vibrant streets of Southampton to the venerable abbeys and later to the peaceful nights spent next to the fireplace.

From the sweet family weekends through the grim lonely Mondays to the endless hardworking weekdays.

From the early childhood years through the freshness of youth to the maturity of adulthood.

From the harsh but promising post-war reality through the carefree 60s and 70s to the roads of self-awareness of the mazy and rocky 90s and 2000s.

From the happy moments of births and marriages to the sorrows of divorces and deaths of loved ones.

From all the good times to all the bad times of which I am sure some of us have had more than a fair share.

From all the highs to all the lows of a bipolar life, a very wavy thing indeed, as life itself can be; through the author's vivid narration accompanied with songs like Spirit in the Sky or Shirley Bassey's melodies in the background, the bipolar myth was demystified.

From the bottom of my heart I want to thank Charles McMullen for the honest, bittersweet time trip he has offered us, I hope that he will return again with some of his future chapters of life, because I think that the best is yet to come.

Miltiadis E Papamichail - October 2013

Introduction

This book describes one man's progress through a life less ordinary. Charles was born into a working-class Hampshire family. He also has bipolar illness and, as a result, has lived a life that was very different from the one he might reasonably have expected. This book describes his 1960s childhood, teenage years and early adult life. It describes the ups and downs of living with bipolar illness, the highs but also the lows and the personal tragedies that have cast a shadow over his life.

I have known Charles for a very long time now and have been involved in some of the events he describes in this book. It gives a hugely interesting insight into one human story behind the label and will be of interest to anyone who knows someone who has experience of serious mental illness - and that probably means all of us.

Dr Steve Brown

November 2013

Chapter One

I drew my first breath on Thursday 24th March 1955 between 2 and 4 am, the same date as Harry Houdini, who like me had a few narrow escapes. I was, so I'm told by my relatives, 'born with a smile on my face'.

The happy event happened in Rookwood Maternity Hospital, Allbrook, Eastleigh in the beautiful county of Hampshire, very close to the River Itchen, which would later be a close friend in my life. This small cottage hospital, finished between 1976 and 1977, is now a residential close called The Paddock.

Ann Maria, Mike and me in the prefab at 32 the Hundred

Ann Maria and me on the beach at Bournemouth

I would later return there on 20th June 1959 with my father in a taxi (we weren't used to such grand transport) for the birth of my younger brother, Michael. A similar place name, Rooksdown, would also feature prominently in my life in another way as you will read later on.

Michael was such a bundle of fun to take home to my older sister, Ann Maria, and my mother, Barbara. In the late 1950s we lived in a prefab, allocated to my dad by Eastleigh Council after he was demobbed at the end of the Second World War. The address was 32 The Hundred, as there were a hundred prefabs on the estate.

The place we lived was right opposite Eastleigh Technical College as it was being built, which is now called Cheriton Road off Chestnut Avenue. Down the way near Fleming Park, near the end of Stoneham Lane, were a few old picturesque thatched cottages which are still there to this day. Our home was quite near to Eastleigh Airport (now Southampton International) where Silver City planes would fly to Paris and open up at the front to let the cars in.

One of my earliest memories is of my Dad lathering up his face ready for a shave and I'm in my pram laughing at him as he plays Father Christmas. Another is of me and Ann Maria eating banana sandwiches with sugar on and drinking junkets (a sweet food made from milk which was popular in the past). After mass on Sundays, Dad would often take me down Nutbeam Road to see the bright red fire engines in their

Ann Maria always kept a close eye on her two younger brothers

Ann Maria's 21st birthday party

Ann Maria and Mike with trike

My first Holy Communion

Me, Mike and Ann Maria at Beaulieu Motor Museum

station. Once we stood at the fence of Eastleigh railway station and saw the Sir Winston Churchill steam engine go past. At three in the afternoon the Bournemouth Belle would rush through with its coffee and cream Pullman coaches, each with a different girl's name on the side.

Once with Dad we both walked up Stoke Park woods in Bishopstoke. The trees were all white, it was very frosty and Dad called it "a very Scottish morning, son". Then one time we were again together by a lock on the River Itchen and he stared into it and said to me, "Still waters run deep, son".

I feel that I was so lucky to grow up in Bishopstoke with its beautiful woods, rivers, parks and old buildings. It even had its own swimming pool run by the local borough council. At the end of every swimming session, Albert Spencer, the lifeguard, would call out over the speaker, "Everybody out now and dressed!" The funny thing was we could hear him saying this over a mile away in Auntie Daphs' garden if the wind was in the right direction!

My mates Tim, Steve, Bob and brother Mike and I all used to climb tall fir trees up the woods, and although we had sticky sap all over our hands and clothes it afforded us a great panoramic view of the planes coming over and landing in Eastleigh airport about a mile away. Super memories!

One time my mates all climbed up the ivy on the wall of the old church tower. Someone dislodged a loose brick at the top and it just missed my head by inches.

One day we went to Cradle Hill in Warminster, as there had been a UFO flap on. A friend of ours, Dave Blunt, his girlfriend and Mike all came along in my old 1962 Austin

Cambridge, which we named "Syd" after its registration plate, SYD 201.

My name was taken from my Uncle Charles, whom I never met as he was lost at sea on HMS *Barham*. He was a patriotic

Dave Blunt, his girlfriend and Mike in "Syd" the Austin Cambridge

Robin Redbreast on wing mirror at Loch Katrine, Scotland

Cousin May with husband Joe in Bed, her children and my Mum

Cousin Margaret with husband Jim and their adopted son

Cousins May and Gerard on right with her children

sailor who once argued with my dad that he was proud to fight for his country, while Dad retorted that he did not like to kill another Catholic. Uncle Charles lost his life at the age of 21. His ship was sunk during the Second World War on 25 November 1941 by the German submarine U-331. Very sad for our McMullen family in Scotland. My Dad's sister Betty had three children, my cousins Margaret, May and Gerard.

One day I remember vividly: snow was falling and had laid a white blanket everywhere – the first time I'd ever seen it – and I asked my mum, "Has the milkman spilt all his milk?" She fondly remembered that story all her life.

One evening a photographer friend of my dad's came round and took a few snapshots of us three siblings on the settee together. We had a little black kitten called Sooty who had one ear bent over and I used to chase her round the lounge and she'd hide behind the sofa. Then I'd ask Mum for the key because I thought she was clockwork.

We had a cuckoo clock in the lounge which cuckooed every hour. Of course I tried to make it cuckoo manually, and broke the damn thing.

On the telly I can remember Richard Baker and Kenneth Kendall reading the news. One programme sticks in my mind, and that was Michael Miles' "Take Your Pick" in which the contestants were asked questions that needed a "Yes" or "No" answer, but if they said either a man would bang a gong and they were out of the game. Once one of our neighbours appeared on the show and we watched him on the telly. Mum told me he was the man she had bought Sooty from.

Incidentally my mother worked in Pirellis' (now known as Prysmian) on Leigh Road in Eastleigh during the war. Its buildings were designed to look like terraced houses from above so that the German bombers would not see it as a factory and therefore ignore it. Mum was a cover girl on the cables. She used to tell us that she worked on PLUTO, which was Pipe Lines Under The Ocean. This massive undertaking stretched from England to France under the English Channel. This would pump oil through for the use of the Allied forces vehicles etc in Europe. There is still a remnant of the cable at Shanklin Chine on the Isle of Wight. Interestingly enough one of the pump stations, at Sandown, was disguised as Browns' Ice Cream Parlour and is still in use today as Browns' Family Golf. Operation PLUTO is still considered to be one of the greatest feats of military engineering history. Good old Mum!

The comedian Benny Hill lived in Eastleigh for a while and worked in Woolworths in Leigh Road opposite the recreation ground with the bandstand. He then worked as a milkman for Hann's Dairies with a horse and cart. That is where he got the idea for the chart topping song, "Ernie". He actually delivered milk in Hamilton Road where I grew up, and today I live not a mile from where he is buried. In Eastleigh on the site of the old Pirelli factory is a road named Benny Hill Close after him.

Back in my youth I had a friend called Michael who looked a lot like the Milky Bar Kid with his national health round glasses on, especially when he dressed up as a cowboy complete with Stetson, guns and holsters for our adventurous games.

When my brother was born Mum asked me what we should call him. I suggested Michael after my childhood friend, as I didn't know many boys' names then.

I also remember one of my sister's friends had a bus driver father who came home for dinner one day with his green and yellow Hants and Dorset bus which he parked outside his prefab. Now the passenger exit and entrance was open all the time, so I sneakily got on and ran upstairs and rang the bell to my heart's content. It's a good job the cab was locked or I would have been playing in there too, steering on an imaginary journey.

Talking about transport, Dad had a motorbike and my sister and I had our photo taken on it with him standing at the front next to his shed, which was an old wartime Anderson corrugated shelter. Dad rode that motor bike to the Esso Refinery in Fawley and back every workday. Later he became a shunter in the Eastleigh Railway Works, where they participated in the dangerous and now banned fly-shunting; they would run along with the trucks and uncouple

Dad with his bike and me and Ann Maria

them manually with a hook on a pole. Then he became ill with his heart and oedema, but he trained as a TV repair man for Rentaset and was learning to drive when he had to retire due to ill health.

My maternal grandfather was born in Channels Farm Road, Stoneham, in January 1899. He lived just half a mile from North Stoneham church, which has a unique one-hand clock. He went to school in what is now the Concorde Club in Stoneham Lane, a disco and nightclub. His name was Frederick George Ball and he was a chargehand boilermaker in the Locomotive Works in Campbell Road, Eastleigh. Fred, as we endearingly called him, suffered from hearing loss as he had clocked up fifty years' service with British Railways Locomotive Works.

He and my grandmother were chalk and cheese. Lillian Rose Goddard was very clean, prim and proper and liked to be grammatically correct. Fred was born in January 1899 and Lil in October 1901 – the year Queen Victoria died. She loved the Royal Family and was a stalwart woman who smoked ten Woodbines a day. She had a friend who used to visit and play whist with her, called 'Mrs Wainwright'. Likewise Mrs Wainwright used to call Gran, in a guttural tone (which I often mimicked) 'Mrs Ball'. People never addressed their acquaintances by their first names in those days.

Every Sunday morning, while the roast dinner was cooking, Gran would dutifully clean the letter box and all the brass ornaments with Brasso. On the mantelpiece above the roaring coal fire was a beautiful ticking clock given to Granddad on his retirement, and sitting by the warm hearth was their long-haired black cat, Dinkie.

Granddad was a great gardener and kept an allotment as well. One area of the garden was "his side" (vegetables) and the other portion was "her side" (roses). Every year Gran would collect all the fallen rose petals for our Catholic Corpus Christi event and we scattered them in Leigh Road Park near the bandstand opposite Holy Cross Church. The church stood in front of the school of the same name at which I started in 1960, and I remember being taught by a steadfast old nun to read and write. Her name was Sister Ann Joseph and her companion was Sister Helena, who was like an angel personified.

We used to use carbolic soap, which smelt strongly of disinfectant. This was good, because the boys used to see who could pee the highest up the urinal wall. At Christmas I played one of the three Kings from the Orient in the Nativity play.

I do recall that all the teachers were women, apart from Mr Andrews and the Headmaster, Mr Delahunt. Sometimes a young priest, Father Michael Peters, would take us down Shakespeare Road Park to play football with us lads. I remember that he still wore his black vestment and clean white collar.

There were quite a few Irish and Polish children there, and now and again there was a fight between them, for which we all crowded around and cheered on who we wanted to win.

My sister was in the last year at Holy Cross while I was there. Then I just saw my brother Michael start in my final year, so I was lucky enough to be at infant and junior school with my elder sister and then my younger brother, but not both at the same time.

Chapter Two

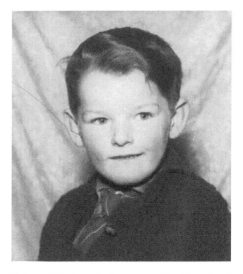

Me in my Holy Cross school tie, wearing Mum's knitted cardigan.

At home things were dire, as Dad was dying and had to sleep on his bed in the front room. I can remember him climbing the stairs on his bottom to get to the toilet. He used to like to hear me read the Bible to him. I asked him how he felt and he answered, "It's like a dagger in my heart, son". The priest came around wearing black and mauve, we said prayers around Dad's bed and the priest gave him his last rites. I recall it was a very sombre moment for us all.

One morning I noticed a lock on the top of the door to where Dad was. I managed to unhook it by standing on the staircase, and entered the room full of trepidation. Inside I saw that Dad's face and body were covered in a sheet. I took a peek at his face and it was white, but very calm and peaceful. It was 23rd September 1962, and my father was dead, at the age of 41.

At breakfast that morning my brother Mike asked Mum where Dad was and she answered profoundly, "He's up with the angels". Mike was only three, I was seven and Ann Maria 12. Our mother was a widow at the tender age of 40.

I looked at my father in the coffin in the front room and gave a nervous, smiling whimper, as my emotions were all over the place. But Mum was an excellent mother. She worked in our school as a dinner lady to supplement her widow's pension and it seemed preferential that we should get second helpings from her. We got our school uniforms on a grant and free school dinners, and Mike had my hand me down clothes and even my bike later on when I'd bought a new one.

Boxing days were great at Auntie Daphne's (Mum's younger sister) and her husband Uncle Ralph. Daph used to like to put on parties using her latest Tupperware plastic food containers.

There were sausage rolls and pineapple chunks on toothpicks with miniature sausages. Even the small triangular sandwiches had little plastic flags on them informing us of their contents, egg, cheese, ham etc. We would have quizzes and I recall she put anagrams all around the room, which I swiftly solved. There were presents under her brightly-lit Christmas tree for the winners. Consequences was another good game we played, along with remembering small items she showed us for five minutes and then hid.

Mike used to like to sing the Beatles' "She Loves You, Yeah, Yeah, Yeah" and Auntie Daph would tape it on her old fashioned double-spooled recorder. Then we'd play it back and have a laugh singing back with it.

Christmas presents I received from Aunt Daph and Uncle Ralph included Spirograph, a David Nixon magic box and *The Guinness Book of Records*.

Daph and Ralph often picked us up in their green Hillman Minx after Mass on Sundays and would drive our family down to places like Lee on Solent, West Wittering, the New Forest and Bournemouth and they would supply the sandwiches and flasks of hot tea and coffee. Great warmer-uppers after a dip in the sea. Once I remember Ralph let Daph drive his Hillman around Stony Cross, a disused wartime airfield. We also got through many an ice-cream cone in those glorious summer days of our lives.

Mum often used to send me up to Uncle Ralph's bungalow with a piece of her special bread pudding for him to take on nights in the railway works. When asked what he thought of it he remarked, "It was OK, but I had a flat tyre by the time I got to work!"

I was very close to Auntie Daph and we had a certain amount of psychic ability. After one of us had said something the other would have been thinking it at the same time. We were both middle children of three, this might have been why we understood each other so well. Between us we could sometimes manage to get the Daily Telegraph cryptic crossword completed together.

After she lost Ralph, we used to travel around together and we once went on a coach holiday to Nottingham. We drove through Sherwood Forest, where Robin Hood and his merry men once roamed, and saw the castle where the

Ralph's Hillman Minx

Uncle Ralph and Auntie Daph

Gran's sixtieth wedding anniversary. L-R back row: Richard, John, Ray, Arthur.
Front row: Me, Patsy, Daph, Ralph, Mum, Ann Maria, Marseilles, Granddad, Granny and Fred

Sherriff of Nottingham lived. Also we went round a factory where they made the famous Nottingham lace.

Mum's youngest sister was called Patsy and she married Ray, but they moved away so we seldom see them, though we sometimes phone and send birthday and Christmas cards. I have two cousins, Richard and Stephen, by them.

When I was five years old we all moved to 174 Hamilton Road, Bishopstoke, in Eastleigh. As I jumped out of the removal van with Mike we both leapt across a front wall and onto a lawn, thinking the building, which looked like a mansion, was all ours. But Mum swiftly told us that we had jumped into our neighbour's garden and that we would be

Silly hats game: clockwise, Uncle Ralph, me, Uncle Ray, stepfather Arthur, brother-in-law John and then cousins Richard and Steven

Granny, me and Mum, St Mary's Church Bishopstoke

Auntie Patsy and me at her wedding

Auntie Daph with me in the garden of Mum's prefab

Me, Mum and Mike watching telly

living in just one quarter of the block.

In my childhood and teens we were very close to Gran and Granddad and we would visit them quite often at the top of the hill at 56 Longmead Avenue. It was built in the 1930s and seemed quite old fashioned to us and large with its pantry, two living rooms, three bedrooms and a toilet, with a bath that had feet on.

Granddad worked a complete eight-hour shift all day in the Boiler Shop of the Locomotive Works during the Second World War. Then during the night he had to go down to Allington Lane at the back of Eastleigh Airport to man the ack-ack guns (anti-aircraft fire). He just used to sleep wherever and whenever he could. The airport was under naval command in 1939 and known as HMS Raven. Spitfires and Lancaster Bombers used the airfield.

Saturday afternoons were a sport ritual with Granddad as he would say "'Ark" (from harken) so that we would all be quiet while he listened to the football results. Fife five, and Forfar so far four. Granny on the other hand liked to watch the wrestlers on TV, such as Mick McManus and Giant Haystacks. She had a great old time cheering and booing them on, especially McManus, who was the "man everybody loved to hate".

She would sometimes get slightly angry with me and say, "Christchurch, Charles!" and I always kidded her that this was her only swear word. When Granddad left the old house in Cranbury Road, Eastleigh he walked all his potatoes from the garden there over to Bishopstoke in a wheelbarrow. Men were men in those golden days.

Granny used to like to watch the horse racing and wrestling on a Saturday afternoon and would give us some paper that bread had been wrapped in to draw on. She also gave us some tracing paper from the stores opposite. Mum worked there when she first left school for Mr Sperring's original shop. Later he was to have many Sperring's newsagents around locally.

One night when we still very young and sleeping in the same bed, I taught Mike to play chess. I did this by holding up the pieces one at a time to the window so that he could see their silhouettes. The next morning I showed him how

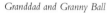

Granddad and Granny Ball

Welcome to "Christchurch" –
Granny's only swear word!

they moved on the board. It wasn't very long before he was beating me at the game!

Ann Maria was a trainee hairdresser and I remember one afternoon on our back lawn she was cutting the grass with her hair scissors for practice. Then later she used to do all our haircuts for free. She liked Shirley Bassey and Andy Williams, especially the ballads. Mum liked Tom Jones' *It's Not Unusual* and *What's New Pussycat?* Alan, our new stepfather, liked all sorts of music, such as Strauss, the Warsaw Concerto, The Dream of Olwen and Flanagan and Allen.

I remember one Christmas when Mike and I slept in Granny's big bed in the back bedroom. It was so cold that in the morning there was an image of a robin in the ice inside the window pane.

When we went down to the front room we discovered to our amazement that Granddad had laid out a round railway track and had an electric steam engine running around on it. That kept us both amused for hours on end.

Granny's blancmanges were lovely. They had corn-starch in them, so they always set to a thick gel. There was always a loud slurping sound as she scooped portions from the bowl. Her pancakes were also out of this world with sugar and lemon on. She also made lovely home-made chips, gorgeous with fish fingers. One day I was eating a packet of crisps when Gran said, "There's nothing in them, I could make more with one potato". So she peeled and sliced one as thin as she could and fried them in a pan. There were more there than a packetful and they were lovely and crisp too.

Me and Mike with monkeys at Weymouth

Ann Maria perming Mum's hair

Ann Maria and me outside Gran's house, 52 Longmead Avenue, Bishopstoke

Me with a football somewhere in the New Forest

Back at home Mum had burnt all the photos of our Dad, as she said she could not live with the dead. All that was left was a red and white chequered black beret with a badge on it and a ribbon down the back. There were also the medals wrapped in greaseproof paper in a neat cardboard box addressed to 32 the Hundred. There was the 1939-1945 Star, the France and Germany Star, the Defence Medal and the British War Medal 1939-1945.

His sister, Aunt Betty, wrote a letter to me from Balloch, Alexandria, Dunbartonshire:

May 25th 2001

Dear Charles,

I have some information re your Dad's army service that has just been given to me. Towards the end of the war the Germans were losing and their Air Force was almost finished. Our government headed by Winston Churchill decided to transfer soldiers from Royal Artillery (your Dad's regiment) to the King's Own Scottish Borderers, known as K.O.S.B. John then served in the 5th Battalion. He served in Holland and Belgium and was in Belgium when peace was declared. He was demobbed in Newton Mearns in Ayrshire, Scotland in 1946.

I hope this information will be useful to you on the internet Charles. I was so glad to obtain this information. His date of birth was 22nd July 1921 and his date of death was 23rd September 1962 aged 41 years.

Good luck Charles in your quest. I'm going to look through my photos to see if I have any army photos of John. Meanwhile I enclose a wee photo of Dad, Ann Maria and yourself.

Bye for now & God Bless.
Love Aunt Betty X

P.S. John Joseph McMullen

I also obtained a letter from the Ministry of Defence which stated that my father was private number 1798872. After enlisting in April 1941 and a lot of different training Regiments including Royal Berkshire Regiment and the Royal Scots, he went on to the King's Own Scottish Borderers, 5th Battalion 15/4/45 and the Argyll and

Sutherland Highlanders, 2nd Battalion 1/3/46. He was discharged from Reserve Liability on 30th June 1959, ten days after Brother Mike's birthday.

Although Dad never spoke of the war, his military conduct was exemplary, of which I am very proud.

Chapter Three

I went to a comprehensive secondary school named Wyvern in Fair Oak. It was brand new in September 1966 when I started there and I can still remember the smell of the newly-laid asphalt on the tennis courts. The playing and sports area was a massive meadow and we could run cross-country in the neighbouring fields and woods, where there was also a lake.

I always rode to school on my blue BSA bike with three speed Sturmey-Archer gears. It needed them to climb the steep Middle Street Hill out of Bishopstoke and up into Fair

1968-69: Back row Martin Davis, Alan Fretingham, Raymond Joslin, Barry Whittaker, Richard Gowans, the author, Roger Bartlett. Front: Tom Jury, Steven Freemantle, Stephen Farmery, Maurice Annals, Geoffrey Hooper, Robert Halley, Eric Anderson, Martin English.

Form Teacher – Mr T. A. Woodford

Oak. Mum always kitted me out clean and smart with a white or grey shirt, red and blue diagonally striped school tie, long trousers and a blazer. On the jacket was a badge with a red winged two-legged dragon with a barbed tail under which the motto was "Advance". In the winter I would ride to school on my bike wrapped up warm in a balaclava and gloves all knitted personally for me by Mum.

The building was ultra-modern for its day and had two storeys, a gym, a hall (where we eventually took our exams and had our meals) and woodworking and metalworking workshops. Outside the biology lab was a goldfish pond. One day someone got pushed in and came out drenched. Ironically, opposite the biology lab was Fair Oak's cemetery.

Although I was no good at French lessons, the teacher, Mr Hardy, was a very nice gentleman who sometimes taught a bit of French philosophy from Voltaire, and Descartes: "Je pense, donc je suis" ("I think, therefore I am").

The Headmaster was Mr Blatchford, who gave me and a few others the cane once for not doing my English homework. We nicknamed him "Scratch", probably because it rhymed with his name. He always started a speech with the sound "Errrr".

The Deputy Head was ex RAF man, Mr Saunders, who was very strict and when he spoke there was instant silence. But during his maths lessons he was quite comical. In one lesson he drew some boys on the blackboard to depict an example, then drew some girls and put the latest miniskirts on them. He had a bald head and on a shiny sunny day we all used to focus our protractors on to his bonce and laugh when he scratched his head.

Our Physical Education teacher was Sam Stevens, who in the late fifties played a few first team games with Southampton Football Club, (the Saints). Every term time he would just write the word 'satisfactory' in most of our reports. After I had left school I saw a photograph of him in the local paper where he was part of the crew for Ted Heath's yacht *Morning Cloud*.

My favourite subject was English language, and I recall I won a book for a story that I'd written. I was quite good at the high jump, ran cross-country for the school and I remember running it in football boots, one of which got sucked off in deep mud.

Two loves of my life I was able to partake of at school were swimming and chess. One evening around 1969 some of us stayed behind and played chess with the Hampshire champion of the time, another ex-RAF man, Leonard Vyne. We didn't have time to complete all the games, but he said that one of us would probably have beaten him. Three would have drawn and the rest of the matches he would have won.

I wasn't too bad at rugby and brought the maths teacher, Mr Coker, down with a great flying tackle. He was quite a big fellow and he just got back up on to his feet and said to me, "Well done, McMullen!"

One fine day we were having a lecture about Christopher Columbus by the rather eccentric history teacher Mr Woodford, whom we called "Woody". Anyway he was telling us that in "Fourteen Hundred and Ninety Two, Columbus sailed the sea of blue" At the same time the geography teacher Mr Morgan popped his head round the door and said, "No it wasn't it was, 'In Fourteen Hundred and Ninety Three, Columbus sailed across the sea'". So now I'm not sure what year it was and which teacher was right!

I did enjoy my Technical Drawing lessons with Mr Sage and remember learning about Orthographic Projections and Parallel Line Developments from him. I actually got so engrossed with my drawing board, dividers and set squares that I was contentedly whistling rather loudly and 'Sage and Onion,' (as we affectionately referred to him) asked if there was a canary in the room. What always made it more exciting was the fact that it was the last lesson of the week on a Friday afternoon and Mum always cooked fish fingers, chips and beans for tea which I always relished at the end of the week. Of course I did not dream then that I would pass exams in pattern development and become a time served engineering tradesman.

During the break times we'd often play football in the wet weather on the tennis courts against the top class. I was in the second to top class right from the start to the finish of my time at Wyvern. I had been borderline with the 11-Plus exam. My sports house was Austen, after Jane, the authoress, and I remember just one other, Keble, after John Keble the hymn writer.

One day during a French lesson a new boy was introduced to the class and I was asked to befriend him. That friendship lasted all through our school days. His name was Roger Bartlett. He was very brainy, often getting 100% in tests. He came from Pinhoe, near Exeter in Devon.

I was friendly and actually quite gregarious with most of the lads in my year.

I remember Mum was invited to the school one evening and in the main hall we were all presented with our "O" level certificates by a local councillor, who I believe was called Mr Pumfrett. Mum was so proud of me that night and so was I.

Today my old school is now upgraded to Wyvern Technology College.

At home as a teenager I had a nice cassette tape recorder when they first came out and I was able to tape all the songs I liked. It had a microphone on it and so I dangled it out of my bedroom window on its long lead and heard Mum and Ann Maria talking in the kitchen.

Nowadays I just download a track from iTunes. We also had a gramophone which Alan Powell provided; he was my stepfather, as Mum had remarried in 1969. I bought a 45 rpm vinyl of *Spirit in the Sky* by Norman Greenbaum, *The Son of Hickory Holler's Tramp* by O C Smith and *Can't Take My Eyes Off You* by Andy Williams, as well as many others.

Alan, being a toolmaker, was very clever with his hands as he was used to working to fine limits, like thousandths of an inch. He stripped out Mum's kitchen with me and Mike and then proceeded to make his own cabinets and cupboards, which he painted and fitted all by himself. At that time he used a lot of Formica (a hard durable plastic laminate) which was in fashion in those days during the late sixties to early seventies. He also knocked a hole in the kitchen wall right through to the lounge, then he built two little hinged doors which Mum served the cocoa through in the evening.

He also built two sheds and one greenhouse in the back garden. All the wood for these came from old disused wagons and were brought home bit by bit on his bicycle over a long period of time. Now that's what I call dedication to a cause. His father had been in the trenches during the First World War, so this type of 'make do and mend' philosophy was engrained in him from childhood.

After a storm the previous night, I rode my bike from school in Fair Oak, to my step-granddad Powell's for lunch as I often did. I noticed that the wind had blown down a corner of his greenhouse which had previously stood for years. He asked me if I would like to repair it for him and I enthusiastically agreed to take on the job.

He got me to take off the top of the wooden bench in his shed and saw it in half lengthways. Then I nailed it together, dug a fairly deep hole in the ground and planted this strong corner pillar in the ground and nailed the sides of the greenhouse to it. Of course this task took me a few hours, so I took the whole afternoon off school. I'm sure Pop thought he was back in the trenches in Northern France.

Inside the sacred tool shop at British Rail Engineering Limited. L-R Uncle Ralph, Les and Alan Powell, (Stepdad), unknown, Ron Herret (Foreman), unknown

Granddad was pleased that his old greenhouse had been salvaged, but Alan wasn't at all happy with me having the afternoon off school as my exams were coming up. He even rode his bike (some six miles there and back) to tell his father off for getting me to abscond from school. I always thought both of them had a good point and that I had learnt a good lesson that day!

Shirley Bassey has been a big hit with me and my sister all through our lives. In June 2003 I took Margaret to Cardiff to see her 50th anniversary show. Margaret noticed her "Goldfinger" coach in the car park of our hotel. I said, "If it's a good enough hotel for us it's good enough for Shirley Bassey." I was emotional during her performance and sang along with her from the balcony. Unfortunately she had to stop the orchestra, but she said the echo was remarkably like herself! Sorry Shirl!

One day, with my neighbourhood friends Steve Stratton and Timothy Cook, I went swimming. We all left our clothes hidden in some bushes, walked up the River Itchen, got in and swam right back down to where our clothes were. Swimming with the current made us all feel like Superman, as one stroke pulled us along like three. Our chests and legs were tickled by the weeds in the river. Brilliant fun!

One day we were considering crossing an electric fence that kept the cattle in the field. Steve thought it would be OK to pee on it, but he got quite a shock in the unmentionables.

Often we would walk south down the River Itchen and along the way the path would be covered with stinging nettles. It was also adjacent to the sewage works, which had once been a Roman villa that had spread right across to what is now Southampton International Airport. We were always glad to get through these nettles and get back into the fresh air, albeit with one or two stings on our legs and arms.

As we ambled on down, we came to a field with cows and a railway bridge for the Eastleigh to Fareham line. We would all shout together under this arch and listen to the booming echo. The path eventually came alongside Eastleigh Airport, where once we were held up by a crazy chap wielding a pellet rifle, but luckily he only teased us for a short while and eventually let us go.

I used to go to the Dell with half a dozen of my mates from school to watch Saints play, and once went down to

Tom Jenkins and Mike Channon.
Two Saints footballers

Stoneham Lane to watch them training, and got all their autographs. Big names then were Mike Channon (England), Ron Davies (Wales) and Terry Paine, the captain.

We always stood at the Milton Road end behind the goal and kept Eric Martin, the goalie, company. Sometimes we'd go to away matches on the train and see the players in their smart suits in First Class carriages travelling to the away ground. Coming back after the game we would talk and drink with them in the buffet bar.

I served my apprenticeship as a sheet metal worker, tinsmith and welder with British Rail Engineering Limited in Campbell Road, Eastleigh. In their own training school I first tried all the different trades to see what I was best at. There was fitting, turning, electrical, sheet metal and carpentry. I was chuffed when I got to be a sheet metal worker, as we had the greatest character for an instructor in Tony Avery. He was very funny at times and used to say when tapping a weld, "That's all it wants, look, that's all it needs".

I once made what is known in the trade as a square to round transformer. I took a great pride in this as I finished and polished all the welds, corners and flanges so that it looked like it was made out of one piece of sheet metal. My mum came with Alan, my stepfather, during a parents' open evening and admired it and told me it looked really good.

The next day my teacher, Bob Avery, told me to throw it out the back in the scrap bin as it had only been a test piece and had no further use. So I did as he asked me and threw it out the back with all the other scrap metal, but I kept on bringing it back into the tin shop as I thought it was too good to chuck out. We all found this highly amusing, including Bob.

Me and my 'tin-basher' colleague, Andy Meaton, made a flue and cowl with a lobster back bend and a wind vane. This was put up over the blacksmith's forge and still protrudes from the roof of the Apprentice Training School to this day. So whenever I go past the old training school with a friend on a train I always show them as we approach Eastleigh railway station from the south and point it out on the right hand side.

The Tin Shop football squad

The lads in the welding school - I'm second from right.

One time we were very naughty and put some oxygen and acetylene in an empty coke can. Then a nipper came along and caused a few sparks arc welding and there was a terrific

*Graham Hutchings, me and Steve Hawks on an apprentices' day outing
to Weymouth. All free on the train of course.*

loud bang as the can hit the roof. We found it later as a
completely flat disc, which Dilly Downs said he'd nail up in
his shed as a memento. It's probably still there to this day.

Some of us boys used to go to the Top Rank Suite discos
in Bannister Road, Southampton on a Thursday night - they
were known as "Peaches and Cream" nights. There were some
beautiful girls there and a lot of them smelt of musk at the
time, which I have always loved. Now and then, if one of us
was getting married, we would have a stag night there.

Even when I was courting Pauline we would go there to
dance on a Saturday night. I worked every day for six whole
weeks to prove to the Building Society that I could earn
enough money to pay off the mortgage on our new house.
This meant working through the weekends as well as all
through the week. So that after work on a Saturday I would

take Pauline down town to the discothèque, dance till about midnight and then fall sound asleep on Pauline's lap till two in the morning when the dancing stopped. How I managed to sleep through all that noise I just don't know, but I was shattered and still managed to get into work later on the Sunday morning. Also we did get the mortgage allowed to us, so it was all worthwhile.

I remember going to the Top Rank ice-skating rink on a New Year's Eve wearing my flashy new red flared trousers. There was a big puddle of water in one particular corner and I slipped and fell right in it, soaking my new trousers. I had to travel back to Eastleigh like this on the bus at one o'clock in the morning of New Year's Day.

At the age of nineteen, for a short spell, I was a member of the Royal Observer Corps in Winchester. While I was there I learned the phonetic alphabet and how to read Ordnance Survey maps. The uniform was a smart blue Royal Air Force type of outfit. Their motto was "Forewarned is Forearmed" (in Latin *Praemonitus Praemunitus*). I did not stay with them for long as I found it enough studying for my City and Guilds exam for my trade.

Later on, during September of 1974, I had a nervous breakdown. My legs would not stop shaking, so I stepped on a live rail in the works yard. The rubber sole on the bottom of my shoe saved my life and it was also a good job that it was a dry day. I was taken to the nurses' station, where my stepfather Alan, and my Foreman, Dick Taylor, came round to see how I was.

The next morning, after the doctor had seen me at home,

an ambulance arrived and took me and Mum all the way to the Rooksdown Psychiatric Wing of Park Prewitt Hospital, Basingstoke. I'd had fears that it would be very Victorian and even thought I'd have to walk a treadmill in there and that it would be like a workhouse. My terror was unfounded, as the place was like a mansion, with four wards, Chester, Wellington (for alcoholics), Chute (which was closed and supposedly haunted!) and Humphrey Owen. I was on Chester Ward, where a nurse told me that the comedian Spike Milligan had once stayed. We had a full sized snooker table on the ward and a grand piano in the lounge.

I remember that one manic patient, Bruce Guest, was an entertainer and had to cancel some of his shows around Christmas time – he was not at all happy with that. Once when Mum was visiting me he played the grand piano for her and asked her to name a song for every letter of the alphabet and he managed to get right through it to the end. A great accomplishment and very imaginative. He was very jolly and cheered up many of the depressed patients even better than what their medications were doing.

One time, while I was playing snooker, I got very agitated and said to a nurse that I would walk the thirty-odd miles back to my home in Bishopstoke. He chased after me with a couple of his colleagues, held me down and gave me an injection to keep me there. They also put me on a section to make sure I stayed and if I tried to escape they would have to ask the police to bring me back.

During our tea meal one day a couple of men were shooting the pigeons to keep their population down.

Medicines were always given to us during mealtimes and the food was pretty good. The grounds were lovely with rose banks and lawns all around.

One charge nurse was called Mr Mills and had an RAF-style moustache. Another senior nurse, who walked the whole hospital and the grounds at night with a torch, was the Irish and very likeable Charley Dolan, who always asked after patients by their first names. We had an occupational therapy shed outside, and this is where we did woodwork and I made a stool with a woven top, as many patients did in those days. Some people made wicker baskets, while others painted pictures. It was always better to go to these groups to help pass the time and meet other patients there. Otherwise it was a long day on the ward just watching the television.

My very first psychiatrist was Dr Guy Mackarness, who was a genial, pipe-smoking, grandfatherly type of a man who had written books - *Not all in the Mind, Chemical Victims* and *Eat Fat and Grow Slim*. He was also a clinical ecologist and had appeared on television and written in newspapers. He understood us well, as he too was bipolar. He was also involved privately in ground-breaking research in clinical ecology.

He had a trolley in his room with different substances like salt, sugar and mustard and would place these on the tongues of his patients and see how they would react. Of course he did all of this privately from his office in Rooksdown and not on the National Health. He had appeared on the telly and written articles for newspapers and magazines, but they would not accept his theories in England so he emigrated to Australia and then on to Canada, where he finally drank himself to death.

He dosed me up with 30mg of Valium a day and it clean cleared the blues away, so that in fact I went the opposite way and had a tremendous high. Then I had to stay in Eastleigh Ward in the main hospital, otherwise known as the ICU (Intensive Care Unit). I only had a week there and then went back to my good friends in Rooksdown. Today they could have got me back down with some Haloperidol but apparently they did not choose to treat me with that drug at that time.

One day I had to have all four of my wisdom teeth out up in Basingstoke at the hospital dentists. They needed to have two anaesthetists to keep an eye on me as I was on so many drugs at the time. They used very small pneumatic chisel guns, so I was told, but I knew nothing about it as I was out cold. Then I had to live with quite a few stitches in my gums, which felt like meat in them which I could not remove with my tongue.

The doctor let me travel back home at weekends on the train and two buses and even paid for my journeys in those days. I spent six weeks in Basingstoke altogether during my first admission and then went back to my apprenticeship in the railway works.

I had experienced some very bad depressions and so once, during another admission, I walked out of the grounds of the hospital and onto the busy Newbury Road. There I wanted to throw myself under a large lorry but could not find the courage to do it. It takes a lot of guts to execute oneself.

I went straight back to the charge nurse on the ward and they soon had me sign a paper for ECT (Electrical

Convulsive Therapy). Every Tuesday morning, with half a dozen other sad cases, I got into the van and we all got driven over to Pinewood Wing. Coincidentally my dear mother had ECT back in 1950 when she experienced post-natal depression in this very same building, but she told us they never put her to sleep in those days for it and she went into convulsive epileptic fits when they put the electrodes to her temples. The nurses put a wedge in her mouth to prevent her from biting her tongue.

Anyway, after my first blast of the 'sparky treatment', I awoke from a very deep anesthetized sleep and felt as if I had been born again. The ward was so lovely and clean and the sun was shining, trying to get through the window blinds that were down all around the room. In fact my first thought was that I had woken up in a spaceship and that the aliens had repaired my mind with this wonderful new treatment. So I went and had this treatment every week for the next five weeks. In all I had 'six of the best' and they did me proud. In fact it blew my depression clean away and left me a bit hypermanic. My memory suffered a little for a few months, but it was well worth it to escape from that nasty old 'black dog' of melancholia.

I continued to make the most of my time in the hospital, and in the evening a few friends and I would go down to the Winkle pub in Winklebury for a few jars and a good old chin-wag and play the jukebox, then have some chips and a pickled onion from the fish and chip shop nearby.

One New Year's Eve, with my brother Mike, we spent the evening in the Swan at Sherborne St. John, which is a seventeenth century thatched pub. We all had a good singsong there but I only drank fruit juices then because of all the tablets I was on. After seeing the New Year in I drove back down the M3 motorway at eighty to a hundred miles per hour, nearly all the time in the middle lane for safety. It was about one o'clock in the morning and there was nobody else about, not even any coppers – thank God. What a terrific buzz that was!

Once back at work I enjoyed the day release once a week to travel with my workmate Andy Meaton and a few others from other firms via St Denys railway station to Woolston, in Southampton where I went to Technical College. We all had a cup of tea in a café which is still there today, even though they took the old floating bridge away from near it and built the new Itchen Bridge. 'Tech', as we referred to it, was in the old Halpins building where Reginald Mitchell had drawn up the plans for the Spitfire. In fact we were told the room where we learned our pattern development was where he had drawn up the blueprints for that aircraft, which had been so important in the Battle of Britain. "Never in the field of human conflict was so much owed by so many to so few," as Sir Winston Churchill had so rightly said during the Second World War.

I do remember one evening that all of us lads had to all make a bowl with a flange around it out of aluminium using a boxwood mallet. When I'd finished mine and had it marked, I took it back and threw it across the River Itchen to see if it would skim across the River Itchen – but it never did. It just floated for a while and then just sank. It's strange to think that this same place was where Spitfires were designed and experimented on as well.

Sometimes on nice warm sunny days we would go down to the Jolly Sailor on the River Hamble at Bursledon and sit on the jetty. We'd have a few pints there and play cards for money, then decide to stay on for the afternoon and not go back to the Tech. At the end of the afternoon we would sign each other's chits with our teachers' names so that we would still get paid for our afternoon of fun.

In the last year we had to take our City and Guilds exams over the river in Southampton Technical College because the builders were pile-driving for the Itchen Bridge at the time and it was too noisy in Woolston to concentrate. Although I cracked up for six weeks, I still managed to make a comeback and pass my exams for sheet metal work and tinsmithing with credit.

A mate, David Blunt, who was a clerk in the paint shop (he is now a psychiatric nurse who does ECTs and depot injections) asked me to pick up a friend and his sister in my first car, an Austin Cambridge. It was built like a tank and was sky blue with a white stripe down each side. We called it Syd after the number plate, SYD 201. A lot of these cars were used as taxis, police cars and even for banger racing which was very popular in the late seventies.

Anyway I picked these people up and took them to the village hall in Lower Upham. It was a great disco for Dave's eighteenth birthday and I danced with his sister Pauline and then split from the hall with her and took her for a quiet drink and chat in the 600-year-old Brushmaker's Arms up the lane in Upper Upham. This is a very interesting old pub with log fires, shaving brushes, brooms and all sorts of sweepers on the walls. It is also supposedly haunted by an old guest who was murdered here, Mr Chickett, who searches for his lost money and belongings in an upstairs room.

Me, Pauline and Mike

Pauline and I then had a very happy courtship in 1976, swimming in the sea at Lee on Solent and walking in the woods up at Farley Mount near Hursley. In fact we were always out and about in my Austin Cambridge around the lanes and villages of Hampshire, spending many an evening in local pubs and restaurants.

We also used to like to go to the cinema. One night in the Gaumont, now called the Mayflower Theatre, in Southampton, they were showing a James Bond film. Roger Moore was gently teasing a bomb to dispose of it when I craftily opened my can of Coke with an explosive hiss. Of course, everybody laughed from the relief of tension.

We exchanged engagement rings on a day out to London along the Embankment. That day we climbed right to the very top of St Paul's Cathedral and enjoyed the expansive, panoramic view from up there. We even spoke to a priest who was sat up there at the top and later on the way down we listened to other peoples' conversations across the whispering gallery.

Both sets of parents happily agreed to the wedding plans. My father–in–law was called Pete, as was his son, and Pauline's sister was called Janet. My mother-in–law, Edna, worked in a café in High Street, Eastleigh called Malc's Mini-Diner. I affectionately called her Eddie Babe - it was just a comical term of endearment.

Chapter Four

After going out together for a year, Pauline and I got married on Saturday 25th June 1977. Just to make sure I wouldn't be without a bride, before Pauline arrived, I asked Janet, her sister and chief bridesmaid, if she would marry me instead if Pauline didn't turn up. She cheerfully replied, "Yeah".

The marriage ceremony took place in All Saints Church, Derby Road, Eastleigh at 3 pm. Pauline wore a beautiful white wedding gown and I wore a sky-blue three-piece suit which I had had made to measure at Burton's and paid a fiver a week for. Mike was our best man and I'd given him Pauline's wedding ring and a cheque to pay off the drivers of our three white Maxi cars. I remember one of the hymns we had was *Now thank we all our God*.

The reception was held close by in a pub and hotel in Southampton Road. In fact it was so near that a lot of people walked to it, while Pauline and I had a tour of Eastleigh in our car (an Austin Maxi) just to show off for a while.

At midnight that night we were permitted as man and wife to board a train at Eastleigh on our first free pass to Weymouth. The train went through part of the town to the Sealink ferry and people cheered us as they saw the carnations in our jackets. We boarded the ferry and sailed through our

*Our Wedding day. All Saints, Church,
Derby Road, Eastleigh*

*Our first wedding anniversary at
Weymouth with a monkey again*

honeymoon night to Grouville, Jersey in the Channel Islands. Next morning we hired a yellow Ford Escort for the week and visited a German underground hospital used during the war and had strawberries and cream on the strawberry plantation. We also had a game of giant chess in Fort Regent in St Helier.

The marriage was a kind and loving one. I changed my job to be a van driver and started delivering parcels for women's catalogues around Salisbury's picturesque villages. The distribution warehouse was close to my home and I had to be there by six-thirty and leave by seven o'clock in the morning. About twenty white Ford Transit vans were in this giant shed and it was filled with exhaust fumes as we all queued up to sign out at the exit doors. Sometimes I had to use an Ordnance Survey map to find a certain farm down a long track through a wood – there wasn't any satellite navigation in those days. But it was all great fun out and about in the fresh air and I certainly preferred it to working in the old Victorian factory.

As I followed tourists on holiday behind their caravans I felt that I was on holiday along with them. It was great to be out in the fresh air and seeing people everywhere contentedly enjoying themselves.

One day I was delivering a parcel to a lady in Gosport, near Portsmouth Harbour, when I looked out across the dock and saw the aircraft carrier HMS *Hermes*, with all the sailors lined up on board standing at ease in their very smart uniforms. They were off to the Falkland Islands and over the loud speakers on board was playing Rod Stewart's *I am sailing*. It was a very memorable and emotional moment for us all.

Pauline worked for Warner Hudnut Lamberts, a pharmaceutical company on Velmore Estate, Chandler's Ford. We managed very well paying the mortgage off for our end-of-terrace home at 32 Whyteways, Boyatt Wood, Eastleigh. It had lovely French windows in the lounge at the back. I recall turning the whole of the garden over and growing a lot of spinach down at the bottom. I also made my own side gate, which I painted light blue and erected myself – I was chuffed with that.

Pauline was a good cook. She made a lovely roast on Sundays and managed a hot meal at the end of our working days too. Our telly at the time had an early remote control, which just went through the channels one at a time and increased and decreased the volume. That was all it did, but we thought it was great not to have to get up to change the channels and volume.

We had a serving hatch between the kitchen and lounge, which was very handy. I've always loved my books and chess, so one year we bought two onyx bookends; they were horses' heads, like the knights in the game of chess.

Once we decorated the lounge with woodchip wallpaper and roller-painted it azure all over. Janet, Pauline's younger sister, helped us and when we had finished we all drove down to Shirley in Southampton and had a Kentucky Fried Chicken in the car. Great fun.

Ann Maria on her wedding day

Ann Maria was married on Saturday October 1st 1977, four months after me. She surprisingly turned up in a two-horse driven cart with Alan alongside her. She looked radiant in her wedding gown and veil with a matching parasol. Everyone enjoyed the service and later the reception in the Memorial Hall down the hill next to the River Itchen. We all had a good dance around together, and then I took Ann Maria and John down to Eastleigh railway station in my little red Hillman Imp. It was a bit of a squeeze, but we made it and saw them both off on their honeymoon.

Later I changed my job again to drive a van for Roboserve, a hot drinks vending machine company. The Ford

Transit was a bit dilapidated. One day the boss sent me to Perivale in London with a load. I got there and while unloading the van the boss there gave me the keys to a brand new three-ton lorry.

I'd never driven anything this size before, but I somehow managed to manoeuvre it through the roads of London and onto the M3. Once I got to Fleet Services for a tea break I was fairly confident with it. I was King of the Road in this vehicle.

Whenever possible I would drop Pauline off at work in the mornings and pick her up in the late afternoon. One night I couldn't sleep as I was excited because I had to go to Wales in the morning, so as Pauline was awake as well we both jumped into the lorry and drove through the night. Luckily when we arrived at 4 am the factory was open for the delivery. Then I drove back and just got Pauline back to work on time. I remember the panoramic view through the windscreen was brilliant, looking all over the tops of cars in front of me and all over the walls to the fields, woods and rivers. Cushtie!

My next-door neighbour was a stonemason, and he was into astronomy in a big way. One night at about 2 am I gazed out of my bedroom window to see him lying on his back on his lawn, looking at the Moon through binoculars.

One January morning I went to work and found, unusually, that my brother Mike was not there. He was a vehicle body builder, hanging the doors on railway carriages. So that lunch hour I rode my bike a couple of miles to Mum's house to find that Mike was comforting her, as Alan had passed away in the night of a heart attack. Mike had tried unsuccessfully to resuscitate him at three o'clock in the morning, but to no avail. Mum was now a widow again, for the second time.

With some of the money from his will I bought a nice fern green Ford Fiesta XL. We all bundled into it whenever we could and went out for journeys and picnics.

After Mum lost Alan I took her to Avington House near Winchester. There was snow on the ground and the lake was iced over. I could hear Mum sobbing in the back of the car, so I stopped and we got out for a stroll around Ovington village. This appeared to settle her down.

One Sunday when Mum was preparing the vegetables for one of her super roast dinners, I decided to go for a drive on my own. I drove through Hursley towards Farley Mount, a high hilltop viewpoint 174 metres above sea level where you can see Salisbury Cathedral in the distance. I noticed a gate was open, so feeling sporty, I drove right on into the woods. I felt as if I was in a rally and drove for miles down and around slippery muddy tracks, until inevitably I got stuck in the mud and couldn't get out. Then luckily I saw two women ramblers who helped me to finally push the car out. I got home OK, but the brake discs were caked in mud.

During work lunch breaks, when we had an hour to spend, we'd sometimes go up the Railway Institute for a pint and a game of snooker. We'd have to run back to work and the first one back would clock us all in, illegally, by 1.04 pm at the latest.

One day I sat in Leigh Road Park on a hot summer's afternoon with my mate Dilly Downs. We'd bought a large bunch of grapes each and ate them all up. What with the heat and this wine we got really quite merry, so we stayed the afternoon there supine and catching a tan near the bandstand.

One day, with our sheet metal instructor Bill Lilley in the tin shop, we had to do some air-conditioning ducting on the roof of the works. It was a lovely May morning as we climbed the ladder with our tools, sandwiches and flasks. During a break from the work we all sat on the roof having our picnics and watching the planes flying into Eastleigh Airport over our heads just like I used to do up the trees in the woods as a child.

Another good job I had was with Reg Lofting, our National Union leader. Again it involved air-conditioning ducting but this time it was in the curtain workshop where all the girls were. We both got a few wolf whistles in there.

Reg was a lovely gentleman and had even been the Mayor of Eastleigh. Our trade union had the longest name of all the unions - the National Union of Sheet Metal Workers, Coppersmiths, Heating and Domestic Engineers.

One day in the tin shop we were repairing train doors and Mick Blacknell had been away for a long time, so someone devilishly covered his door in weeds. We all had a good laugh when he eventually came back and we were all hammering our hammers and mallets in unison to chide him on.

We made our own stainless steel kettles and boiled them up with water on the gas-soldering iron burners. There were about five different tea schools for about thirty odd men. Tea breaks were 9-9.25 am and 3-3.25 pm and we'd all read the papers and try and get the *Sun* crossword done between us.

Of course Reg Lofting (our shop steward), being a brainy bloke, did the *Daily Telegraph* cryptic crossword and I do recall that in the rainy dinner hours he made a beautiful swan-necked copper kettle. He was a lovely bloke. Also he was the President of our Union, the National Union of Sheet Metal Workers, Coppersmiths and Domestic Engineers – the longest-named Union in the UK.

We had to cut the sills off the bottoms of the carriages because of rust. There were two of us doing this, one each side, and each pneumatic chisel gun was 120 decibels each, so the total noise was at a highly illegal level. The air was cold and wet coming out of the hosepipes. We wore Martindale face masks, cotton wool in our ears, earmuffs (you couldn't even get Radio 1 on them), goggles and cotton and leather gloves. Some of the lads used the triangular sling bandages from the first aid cupboard in the coaches to use as mufflers to keep the dust out of their mouths.

For a little while I worked down the bottom of the yard with a few other lads in the asbestos house. We had to wear yellow BIG suits (Biological Insulation Garments) and we looked just like spacemen in them. We had to cut out panels and vacuum all the asbestos out, sometimes white and sometimes blue – the worst one.

You could choose to have your air filtered through a pack on your side or from a tube which came in from outside the specially-built workshop. I chose the latter way. You could only work for two hours a day in there, so the rest of the time was spent drinking tea, chatting and playing games. A shower was taken after the work was done and we cleaned each other's BIG suits off while still in them, then showered our bodies off. Even the underwear was supplied by the railway.

Later I had a trial as a finished work inspector, where I could wear my wedding suit to work. It involved a lot of signing papers, so I was glad I didn't get the job and was happy to return to the tin shop with my old mates.

One day I left work and when I got home I found Sam outside my house to meet me. He was my CPN (Community Psychiatric Nurse). He asked me and Pauline to get into his car and drove us straight up to Mum's house in Surrey Road, Chandler's Ford. When we got there we found Mum crying, but very pleased to see me.

Then Sam told me that earlier that morning Mike had leapt off the Itchen Bridge in Southampton to his death. It was September 1st 1980.

I was devastated. While I waited and consoled Mum, Granny and a neighbour, Mrs Wilson, were there too. Eventually Dr Margaret Tansley came and told us all not to reproach ourselves over this tragedy. This was a very solemn time for all of us. Later that evening I took Mum over to Bishopstoke to visit Ann Maria and her husband John.

Life was never the same for us after losing dear Mike. But on his grave we had inscribed "To live in the hearts we leave behind is not to die", From Thomas Campbell's *Hallowed Ground*.

Mike was only 21 years old. He had had a good life, though a very short one. He left behind a girlfriend from Syria called Diana, who was going to Southampton University. He had written a letter to her father asking for her hand in marriage and this was romantically placed in the coffin along with the engagement ring.

Chapter Five

Mum was now living all alone, so one day Ann Maria and I got on to BT and bought her a phone, something she had never had before. On the day it was to be installed Ann Maria stayed in at Mum's place while I took her for a drive with Pauline down to Lee on Solent. I went round the block first and from the end of Mum's road I just managed to spy the BT van outside her house.

Later Mum got married again, for the third time, to Arthur Frank Chatterton Bailey. He was now my third 'father' and second stepfather. I left my trade as a sheet metal worker and became a van driver for Littlewoods women's catalogues. I delivered mainly to the country villages around Salisbury. One I remember had the price of bread over the years written in stone on the wall of St Giles' Church, Great Wishford in Wiltshire.

As if losing my brother wasn't enough, Pauline put in for a divorce. I got depressed and ended up in Rooksdown, Basingstoke again. Then I lost

Ann Maria

54

my job and my house - all five top stressors at one time. I don't know how I coped with it, but with the help of my dear friends on the ward and my very close family, somehow I pulled through it all. When I came out of hospital Mum let me live with her and my second stepfather Arthur.

Mum saw an advert in the *Echo* for a kitten, so I went down to Highfield and bought this beautiful wee cat. The young lady who had him had called him Bonington after the mountaineer, Chris, as he was always climbing trees. So I took this little bundle of joy home and we eventually shortened his name to "Bonnie". He was a tortoiseshell tiger tabby. He was a super cat and a right funny little character. We'd take him out with us in the car for runs and just treated him as one of the regular members of our family.

Bonnie on the roof of our shed with next door's cat

Mum and Bonnie at Lee on Solent

Bonnie in the kitchen

I often walked him on the beach at Lee on Solent and if a dog came along I'd pick him up, or he'd just walk back to the car. He absolutely loved his freedom there and benefited from the briny as we did. He seemed to love it on the pebbled beach next to the expansive coastline. The local ice cream man always put a fresh bowl of water out for Bonnie.

By now I'd sold my marital home and had purchased a lovely ink-blue Triumph 2000 TC, which was quite plush and had armrests in the middle, front and back.

One fortnight we drove down to Westward Ho! for a holiday. Mum and Arthur travelled free on the train as Arthur was a train driver. I took all our luggage in the large boot and Granny sat in the back with an empty seat each side of her. Granddad sat in the navigator's seat alongside me and Bonnie the Super Cat roamed around wherever he wanted too. Sometimes he was up around the steering wheel with me, but a lot of the time he just slept in the footwell by Granddad's feet, where it was warm and dry.

As soon as we got to the caravan we opened the car door to let the cat out and he ran straight into the cornfield next to us and chased a field mouse. He retrieved it and brought it to our caravan. He must have thought it was a gift for us, that funny little feline hunter.

When we arrived back from a day's outing Mum would strike a Swan Vesta match in the dark and the smell of the sulphur fumes would precede those of the Calor gas which she then lit at the mantles to illuminate the caravan. A very memorable olfactory and visual moment!

I do recall that the Poet Rudyard Kipling went to school

The village in Devon that's named after me   *...and the McMullen barracks at Marchwood.*

at Westward Ho! and that each pebble on the beach is the soul of a lost mariner – so legend has it.

We visited the villages of Charles in North Devon and East Leigh in South Devon and I had my photo taken at each place for posterity. We learned from speaking to a local that a big articulated lorry once turned up in this small village called East Leigh. The driver had got Eastleigh in Hampshire mixed up with its North Devon namesake!

At the end of the holiday Mum and Arthur took a taxi to the railway station while we loaded up the car. Before he left, Arthur, Granddad and I all went to the gents' toilet before the long journey back. Mum and Granny naturally went to the Ladies. As we stood at the urinals relieving ourselves, who should walk into the gents but Bonnie the Cat. He must have known he was a little boy!

On the way back we stopped off at Ottery St Mary, as Granny knew she had a relative there somewhere and also the poet Samuel Taylor Coleridge had lived there. Granny's memory was a bit vague and she couldn't remember where her long-lost country cousin lived. We let Bonnie off his lead to have a stroll round but he didn't come back for at least half an hour. He must have met a nice little girl cat.

As I settled down after my decree absolute I started to date a young girl of eighteen - I was twenty eight. Her name was Debbie and she lived in a convent home. She had been learning to be a vet and of course she loved our Bonnie. One night I sneaked her into my bed, unbeknown to Mum and Arthur. We got up at about five o'clock to avoid Arthur seeing us before he went to work. Then we drove down to Bournemouth in my Triumph. I took some lovely photos of Debbie on the beach as the sun was rising.

One day we went to the Royal Victoria Park at Netley and walked down to the military cemetery through a long dark tunnel of trees. Later we put up a tent for the afternoon in the grounds of the old hospital. It poured with rain, but it was nice and cosy and good fun inside.

L – R Granny, Mum and Debbie   *Debbie at Bournemouth*

Me and the River Itchen

*Me with backpack starting
another walk*

*Me sitting at Alfred Lord Tennyson's desk,
Farringford House, Isle of Wight*

I used to walk about fifteen miles every other day out and around the Hampshire countryside on footpaths with an Ordnance Survey map walk and compass. Sometimes I'd get a train or bus to Winchester and walk back down my old friend the River Itchen to Bishopstoke, not needing a map or compass, just dreaming and experiencing the beauties in life.

When I was up at Cheesefoot Head, a very high point, I was caught in a ferocious thunderstorm. I got drenched through to the skin. Eventually the sun came out and I stripped off all my clothes and hung them in the branches of a tree while I had some sandwiches and coffee from my flask.

By the time I'd finished my lunch break my clothes were lovely and warm and dry. So I got dressed and carried on my walk, but not before I had promised to buy myself a good

Gore-Tex anorak and leggings, which I did in the next few days in Blacks at Fareham, as they were the nearest local outdoor gear shop to me in those days.

I went into Rooksdown again and this time I was under Dr Paul Bartlett, who diagnosed me as manic depressive, now known as bipolar. It felt a relief to me and my family to know what was wrong with me and that others suffered from the same condition. An awful lot of famous people have suffered with this disorder such as Spike Milligan, Stephen Fry, Elizabeth Taylor, Buzz Aldrin, Lord Horatio Nelson, Bach, Beethoven, Blake, Churchill, Dickens, Thomas Edison, Elgar, Goethe, Handel, Victor Hugo, Keats, Kipling, Abraham Lincoln, Liszt, Michelangelo, Mozart, Mussolini, Napoleon, Isaac Newton, Poe, Rachmaninov, Roosevelt, Rossini, Schumann, Shelley, Tchaikovsky, Tennyson, Tolstoy, Turner, Van Gogh, Wagner, Watt and Woolf. The list goes on, but these were all extraordinary people and geniuses in their fields. These people were great not in spite of their illness, but because of it. Bipolar disorder often appears in art, music, literature, poetry, science and philosophy. Many manics do not reach their peak, but it is often found among the poets and leaders of this world.

Manic Depressive Psychosis is unpredictable, with its anxious mood swings from high to low and back again, torturing not only the sufferer but their loved ones. They say it is caused by many traumas in life or biochemical or from an inherited gene. But this is all too technical for even the doctors, let alone this book.

I only know the agony of a severe low mood when I can't

get out of bed in the morning and would sometimes even stay there until two or maybe three in the afternoon. At least I felt safe wrapped up in my little cocoon. But this could last for two or three days and be quite serious, with thoughts of harming myself or even suicide. Sometimes an ambulance needs to be called, and I am taken to Southampton General Hospital where they keep an eye on me for a few hours and then I get a taxi home usually in the early hours of the morning.

After all this rest I might get an energy surge and stay awake for two days and two nights right through. This nearly always leads to a manic attack when I feel I could do anything – quite the bipolar opposite of a lethargic depression. "How great the change from major to minor", as the lyrics of the old song go.

Occasionally, during the winter months with their short dark days, I suffer from SAD (Seasonal Affective Disorder). This makes me very tired and lethargic and again I just want to sleep all of the time. I have a SAD lamp which mimics the brightness of a sunny day and this helps me to cope in the morning while I am having my breakfast.

I might also get a bit of agoraphobia and have to push myself to get out of the front door. I find it helps to take deep breaths before I leave the house, and then once outside, things don't appear so bad. It's just a matter of going in and out of the front door, then I feel free and fairly confident again. I might just begin again with a short walk to the local shops or to the library. Every journey begins with the first step.

One of the worst aspects of my condition is sociophobia, which leaves me very shy in the company of more than one person, usually strangers. In the main I quite enjoy living in isolation with it either dead quiet or with a bit of music in the background. I live almost like a monk with a vow of silence, as I only see people when I go out on the buses to various local towns or the odd train journey a bit farther afield. On the whole this quiet lifestyle suits me a treat, as I prefer to work alone and undisturbed.

One day, when I was staying in Park Prewitt mental hospital in Basingstoke, I washed Dr Bartlett's white MG sports car off. As I finished it off I emptied the bucket of muddy water over the rear of it. The next day I asked him how he liked his clean car and he replied, "It's all right, but it looks like a cat walked over the back of it".

Park Prewitt was a fine Victorian style complex of buildings, but alas it has been closed and is now a housing estate. The new 'care in the community' has taken over and they also refer to it as 'hospital treatment at home'. There aren't many beds in the new psychiatric hospitals and there aren't enough Social Workers, Care Co-ordinators and Registered Mental Nurses to cover the vast numbers of mentally ill patients in their homes.

I met Maureen White while I was in Rooksdown and we remained good friends for about a year after we were both discharged from hospital. She was ten years older than me and we used to go to the cinema every Friday night. She had a little scooter and used to travel from Rownhams to Bishopstoke to visit me, when Mum would let her stay for tea. Friday night was always our cinema night and we enjoyed many a good film and pot of popcorn together.

We'd go for walks in the woods and around the fields near the M27. At this time I was very interested in doing the cryptic crossword in the *Echo*. As luck would have it her father kept hundreds of these old newspapers in his garage, and Maureen would cut out half a dozen at a time for me to solve.

It was also about this time that I sat three Mensa IQ tests, the first at home, the second at the University of Portsmouth, then finally at London University. My score was 146 (superior intelligence) – not bad when the national average is 100 and I only went to an ordinary comprehensive school. "Hampshire be I born and bred, strong in the arm and thick in the head."

At this time I was also attending Bedford House, a day centre in Amoy Street off Bedford Place, Southampton. Sue Law used to take us out in a Ford Transit van down to the New Forest and around and about Hampshire for healthy walks. There was Pottery and Art, Woodwork and Metalwork and different types of psychology classes. We had fresh meals cooked in the Arts Café every day.

Once a year we would go on holiday with the club in their own light blue Ford Transit. I remember one year we went to Mid Wales, to a place called Dolgellau near Barmouth Bay. After a few leisurely days and one of climbing the foothills of Snowdon, six of our best walkers, including me, were chosen to climb Cadair Idris. We went up with a mountain rescue man with a coil of rope on his shoulder and his dog Peris – named after a Welsh saint. After climbing up a giant staircase, the wind was too cold and was giving some of us a bad headache. So at two thousand feet the rescue chap said that we would have to abandon the climb and told us to descend the mountain. At least we all got to climb two-thirds of it.

Its height is 2,930 feet and it is said in folklore that if you sleep on the mountain you will either end up a genius, a madman or a poet.

Those who couldn't climb the mountain were taken to Barmouth on the estuary of the river Mawddach and Cardigan Bay.

After a very pleasant week there, on the way back home to Southampton, I navigated for the manager in his car and got him to take a long, straight 'B' road, unlike those in the Transit van who went on the motorway. Strangely enough we never saw them again on the journey until we passed them on The Avenue which leads into Southampton. Of course we all cheered and waved to one another as we passed.

Back at the club one fine day, at a members' meeting, I heard the beautiful voice of a young lady laughing heartily, so later I asked if she'd like to take a cup of tea with me in the garden and listen to my Elvis cassette on my ghetto blaster. She agreed and I said to her, "When are you going to invite me round for tea then, Margaret?" To which she replied, "You can come round tonight if you like, but I haven't got much in."

So at the end of the club, at about 3 pm, we jumped into my little red Lada and went round to Roy's, her local corner shop, where she got some provisions in and made us a lovely little tea meal.

She had a nice clean, fresh and roomy upstairs flat at 27A Marchwood Road, Freemantle. I remember well that she had a very healthy fern plant in a pot on a white embroidered cloth on a small coffee table. The place was very clean, uncluttered and airy.

Margaret was a very young and vivacious 46 and I was a mere 32 on Tuesday 9th September 1986 when we met. Despite the 14-year age gap we were to get on very well together for the next twenty one years. We went on holiday in a caravan down to Overcombe camp site near Weymouth in Dorset. It was next to the River Jordan, where John Constable the artist had his honeymoon. While there we realised that Margaret had a slight bump in her tummy – yes, she was pregnant.

Early on the first morning we walked up above the campsite to visit King George III on horseback, a carving on the chalk hill above Overcombe, but he looks more like Sherlock Holmes wearing his deerstalker hat. This wonderful view can be seen across Weymouth Bay from the beach with its lovely fine, almost white sands.

Another day I had a swim in Portland's swimming pool and then we had cheese rolls high on a hill, at Fortuneswell, watching the naval ship and helicopter movements.

Of course we also went into Weymouth itself to do some shopping and walked along the promenade along the bay with its lovely white fluffy sand. I have lovely memories of us eating fish and chips sitting in deckchairs on the beach soaking up the sun.

My old Lada seemed to hold out during the duration of that holiday, although it had some incurable electrical problems. When we got back home the exhaust fell off and it sounded like a racing car with no silencer. Very embarrassing!

I left Mum and Arthur to settle in my own bedsit at 27 Waterloo Road, Freemantle. I was into betting on the horses in those days and I measured that I was just five furlongs from my own 'filly', Margaret, otherwise known as five eighths of a mile or just over half a mile. Anyway I usually rode my bike downhill to her place and locked it up in her shed.

My bedsit was comfy and warm in the winter and as cool as a cathedral in summer, because it faced north. However this meant I did not get any sunshine in my room, which was not good for my SAD (Seasonal Affective Disorder). Albert, the landlord, said that I was his best tenant as I was hardly ever there, so I did not wear out his carpet and other objects in the bedsit. On the other hand most of my week was spent at Margaret's flat, which had a balcony at the back looking over the container port. I'd often sit outside there and do my crosswords while Margaret sang to me while hanging her washing out on the line. It was a glorious sunspot.

Sometimes after visiting my sister in Bishopstoke, Margaret and I would go and watch some amateur dramatics in the Memorial Hall just off the River Itchen. Some of them were very funny indeed, some were whodunits and there was always tea and cakes during the interval. We would often have to leave early to get the last bus back to Southampton. Margaret did enjoy these trips out, especially when she was in her wheelchair in the latter days of our relationship.

Just opposite the hall was a very small car park by the river, and when we had the car, we used to sit there and eat our fish and chips while listening to the radio or music on a CD. I would reminisce to Margaret about when I used to paddle in the river there as a young boy. One day I trod on an eel and it slithered away under my bare foot. It was a very eerie feeling and sent a shiver down my spine. Also sometimes a fire engine would park there and put a hose into the river and refill its tank.

In Freemantle, in Southampton, I had a lovely bedsit landlord called Albert Norwood, who came from Waterford in Eire. He once took me for a drive down to the New Forest, to Hatchet Pond, where a lot of children fly kites and model aircraft and boats.

One Easter we went to a service at Winchester Cathedral and afterwards we shook hands with the Bishop outside this massive building, which has the longest Gothic nave in Europe.

It was sometimes hard for Margaret and me to live together with both of us suffering from manic depression, and neither of us working. But we also couldn't live without one

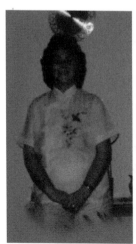

Margaret in her pyjamas   *Margaret and me at Christmas in her flat*

Margaret

Me with my bedsit landlord, Albert Norwood

another. So we were together most of the time, just like a couple of pensioners with plenty of time on our hands as I wasn't working then. Sometimes we would squabble and the police were summoned to what they called a domestic dispute. But through it all we loved each other intensely, especially if we were both high, and we'd stay up all night round the gas fire philosophising, cracking jokes, singing, dancing, laughing and reminiscing. Margaret had a great voice and sounded almost exactly like Ella Fitzgerald.

I like to sing ballads such as *The Green, Green Grass of Home* and some of Mario Lanza's songs such as *The Lords' Prayer* and *I'll Walk with God* as well as the ballads of Tony Christie. Also I'd sing along with Celine Dion and Whitney Houston. I like to try to emulate in Italian with Russell Watson and Lulu with *The Prayer* and *O Sole Mio*.

Now I have a favourite app on my iPad called Shazam Encore and it hears a song and then comes up with its lyrics. Magic!

Early in the morning of Sunday 13th September 1987,

Margaret gave birth to a very healthy baby girl. I was in attendance at Princess Anne's Maternity Hospital at the birth and as soon as I saw my daughter Margaret asked me, "What do you want to call her?" I replied after a little thought, "Serena". She observed how much the baby resembled my sister. It was so lovely to hold her in my arms. The name means calm and tranquil, as in the wind and the sea. Beautiful! She was, and I sincerely hope still is.

So now Margaret had three sons and three daughters. Three boys, Peter, Eddie, and Paul and a girl, Caroline by her marriage and another girl, Natalie by someone else.

My Mum and Ann Maria came down from Bishopstoke to visit us three and see the new baby, but unfortunately so did Dr Chris Nunn, who diagnosed Margaret with post-natal mania. He wanted Serena moved to a cottage hospital down at Lyndhurst in the New Forest called Fenwick, while Margaret was placed in the Department of Psychiatry (DOP) in Southampton and given tablets to dry up her milk so that she wouldn't bond too closely to Serena, who we saw every couple of days when a social worker brought her around to us.

When Margaret was discharged we were allowed to have Serena back, but it was only until the social worker could find foster parents. Once found we could only have the baby for a few hours a day and we used to go out for journeys in the car down to the New Forest and Bournemouth etc. Ambivalent times for all three of us.

It seemed cruel to all of us in our newly-made family as the social worker took her away at the end of each visiting day and then brought her back another day for our outings together. We referred to them as the KGB, as we were innocent people, guilty only of being bipolar. Margaret was a very good mother and provided all the needs of our new baby.

After a while of this toing and froing I developed post-natal depression myself and took an overdose of Largactil at my mum's one weekend. It was during the very bad storm of October 1980. I went into a coma and had my stomach pumped in Winchester County Hospital. When I came around I thought I was in Heaven as it was all so white, clean and clinical, and I remember a male nurse giving me a strict telling off.

Next morning I saw Dr Morris, a lovely lady psychiatrist, who admitted me back to Rooksdown in Basingstoke once again. Later in life I would attend Morris House, which she helped to start. More on this later.

The Wait

How is my love when she's alone?
Miles apart and doesn't phone.
Where is the justice that lets us pine?
Is the pain hers and also mine?
Why does distance keep us apart?
One from t'others counterpart.
When will our meeting time allow?
Fate and action, mixed somehow.
The passion of action forces this:
To enjoy a worthy, heartfelt kiss!

Lovers must feel both pain and pleasure,
Which time and distance cannot measure.
Expect love, it may not be there;
Run from it and it will dare
To chastise and win you back,
It goes like that, it has this knack.
When it flows smooth as a valley's stream,
Sly destiny knows its cunning scheme.
Ethereal threads bond it together
To sway around in all types of weather.
Love can return with a sparkle,
Like Mr Hyde and Dr Jekyll.

Chapter Six

Among other memories I have of the old psychiatric wards are the great big long corridors where you could walk off anxieties and meet people and the Creole nurses who would play games with us like chess and talking therapies. I made many a good friend among the patients, visitors, staff and doctors.

One time I was walking through the grounds of Park Prewitt with a gay chap and a psychopath, as you do. As we neared our ward the psycho picked up a branch that was lying on the ground under a tree and cracked it over the head of the gay guy. I'll never forget the sound of the crack and the yelp that the attacked chap let out!

On a lighter note, I met a manic who got me to download *Shaft* by Isaac Hayes on my iPhone. Every time this certain Afro-Caribbean patient marched through the ward we would play it full volume. It was so funny we were in hysterics and often had belly-laughs together till the wee small hours of the morning. The night nurses didn't like this much, as they had been trying to get us to bed since midnight.

Sometimes we'd just sleep on the couches for a few hours and wake up ready dressed on the ward and ready for our breakfasts. The bedrooms on Wessex Ward in Antelope House are very good and have single beds with a shower room as well now, unlike the old hospitals, like Knowle near Fareham and Park Prewitt near Basingstoke both in Hampshire. Then there was the Old Manor in Salisbury, Wiltshire. These had large dormitories and long hallways to walk up and down, but they both had beautiful large grounds and gardens which some of the patients tended to. Knowle Hospital even had a farm on the campus.

By far the most modern and splendid hospital I ever stayed at was Woodhaven at the Tatchbury Mount site near Cadnam in the New Forest. I was taken there in a police van, as I had stepped into the road in front of a car. I was really just mad about the amount of traffic on our roads at the time. They thought I had tried to commit suicide, so I was taken there on a thirty-day section. They had different staff for the patients every day, psychiatrists and psychologists at the ready to consult with during one's stay. The food was cooked fresh on the premises and was always delicious, and you could often get second helpings there. Even the doctors sometimes ate with us in the same room.

Outside, the gardens were a sylvan paradise with trees, shrubs and flowers all around. Having a big garden was a good thing for me as I was on that section for a month, and so was quarantined in its environs. As I was taken there promptly by the police, arriving there at one o'clock in the morning, I had not been able to pack a case and was just in the clothes that I stood up in. The staff soon kitted me out with some spare attire which they had in a cupboard for on the ward, and there were washing machines and dryers on the premises. I enjoyed my stay there and was studying the poetical works of Percy Bysshe Shelley at the time. I remember fondly using the internet on my newly acquired iPhone to copy out *The Skylark*, *The Moon* and a few others.

An old man who resembled Albert Steptoe, a young girl and her American boyfriend from the Mid-West and a few others used to all sit around together at a picnic table. I had many a good few games of chess on that table with 'Steptoe'. During the games we discovered that we were both as crafty as each other. The winning and losing was about even. We stayed out there all day during that glorious July of 2011, soaking up the sun and getting high on each other's jokes. As the evening crept in the lights would come on and illuminate the leaves on the shrubs and turn their colours into a beautiful transparent yellow. With such lovely, funny company and great surroundings it was just like being on holiday there. Unfortunately they closed Woodhaven in 2012, at a great loss to the mentally ill people who used it and of course its staff.

After a manic outburst I was taken in a taxi with a male nurse to Wessex Ward at Antelope House, the psychiatric hospital in Southampton at the Royal South Hants complex. I remained there on good behaviour and was discharged a week before my section ran out.

One time at about midnight, after the people on the ward had gone to bed, a chap was ranting and raving at the top of his voice for ages, so the charge nurse played some music very loudly through the ward speakers. This drowned his booming soliloquy out and he soon became quiet again and went to bed.

We would have formal ward rounds with our consultant psychiatrist and a nurse and social worker would be present. Sometimes family members attended these meetings. Drugs were reviewed and time to go on leave or a complete discharge was arranged.

Once in hospital I recall that I posted my disabled railway pass down to Margaret so she could travel up to Basingstoke to visit me cheaply. Within a few days she came up and looked radiant in a French bright blue beret. She told me how much she and Serena missed me. It wasn't long after that that I was discharged and back home with my loved ones where I belonged, to have a nice Christmas together. It wasn't until Easter of 1998 that Serena was taken away from us and adopted. This was because Margaret was a bit too old at 47 to cope with the baby and we both suffered from bipolar, which added to our burdens.

In the last few years I received a letter from Serena and she firstly mentioned that she "turnt out all right" (sic). I was so pleased to read this as I was concerned that she might have had a double bipolar gene from her mum and myself.

She tells me that she has a little boy (so I'm a Granddad myself now) but I don't know his name and whether she is married or not. She tells me she would like to enter the police force one day, which is strange, because I wanted to be a detective when I was at school. She also told me that she likes the singer Mariah Carey and wanted to be famous like her so that I would see her and know that she was all right.

In the same vein I would like her to maybe hold this book and read about her Dad's life story. The only other thing I know is that the letter came from the social work department in Ipswich, Suffolk. I wrote to her some years ago and included my address and phone number so that she might one day contact me directly instead of through the system. I am waiting to hear from her to this day.

I had a little red Lada car and Margaret and I continued to rove around the local counties in it. I had the "nerve of Old Nick", as Margaret used to say as I drove into the grounds of Mottisfont Abbey on a day it when it was officially closed. We drove right along the River Test path inside the grounds and waved to a monk on the way out. I don't know who he thought we were.

We also drove around Cranbury House, Hursley, near Winchester and Broadlands, Romsey, where we waved to a gang of gardeners with spades and wheelbarrows. When we drove through Avington House on an ordinary autumn day we passed a posh lady (probably the owner) and her friend sweeping up some leaves. She said, "What are you doing in here?" so I drove on through. Luckily for us the gates were open at the other end of the estate for us to make our crafty escape. We always got away with these trespasses and people said we must have had charmed lives.

One morning I had a parcel delivered. I didn't open it until I had picked Margaret up and travelled to the village of Chawton, near Alton, where we parked opposite Jane Austen's house in the pub car park there. Then we sat on a park bench together where I unwrapped the parcel with great excitement. It was a well wrapped-up computer chess set. It was a very windy day and all the small polystyrene packing pellets blew all around the village. It looked like snow everywhere in the gutters and all over the lawns and the lane. As I was picking up the pieces one by one a lady passed me by on a horse and said to me, "That's a very socially aware thing you're doing". I don't think she realised I had spilt them in the first place!

I often like to go for a constitutional walk to help keep me fit and keep my weight down. So I get the bus up to Rownhams and walk back home. It has nice old houses up there with horses and cows in fields and plenty of woodland and countryside. If I am lucky someone has a bonfire on and I love the smell of the fires in the air. This confirms I am out of the city and into the countryside like where I grew up.

I was quite outgoing and had plenty of friends in my youth and mid years. But now that I am in my late fifties I do not crave for much human company. I suppose you could say that I am now a bit of a loner and feel quite happy on my own with my many pastimes.

One hobby I do like very much using my iPad. I love to watch "The Beverley Hillbillies" and "I Love Lucy" shows from the sixties and fifties on "You Tube". I find Jed Clampett is so naïve about his new mansion and city ways compared with his old lifestyle in the mountains. He even calls his swimming pool the 'cement pond' and he is amazed that every time he hears the doorbell chime there is somebody at the front door! Granny, Miss Elly, Jethro and the banker, Mr Drysdale, were all so well cast in these hilarious comedies.

When I am manic I spend a lot of my savings. I might buy, for instance, a shortwave radio and the aerial to go with it. I would buy various books about it with the frequencies in lists. Then in a couple of years' time I've had enough of it and I would sell the radio for a big loss at Cash Converters and give the books to charity.

Once I bought a VHF/UHF scanner and I had a sixteen foot pole with a discone aerial erected on the side of my house for it. With this special apparatus I managed to pick up the communications between the Red Arrows air display some thirty odd miles away in Bournemouth bay. Then I found to my dismay that the aerial was flapping in the wind and causing an eerie noise inside the house, so I had to pay out again to have that removed.

I also enjoy buying lots of books and collecting them. This is known as bibliomania or bibliophilia. I have, for example, twenty-four different crossword solving books with lists of mountains, rivers, prime ministers, battles etc. I like to read them and some teach me how to do cryptic crosswords and I enjoy the riddles and double entendre meanings and puns in them. Just recently I had to have two new shelves put up in the lounge to accommodate them all. I already had one other shelf and a bookcase full of other books in the lounge and I also have another long bookshelf full in my bedroom. I sincerely hope that I don't end up with them all up the staircase and across the floor as some eccentrics do.

Somehow I manage to keep my small house in order, and once a fortnight a lovely lady called Kim comes around to do my cleaning. She is very thorough and we always have a good chat and a laugh together. Strangely enough her father was a sheet metal worker for the old bus company of Hants and Dorset, which was the same trade as I have.

One of the biggest mistakes I ever made with my money was to buy a lovely white electric bike with all the accessories like panniers, lights, stirrup pump, water bottle and even a digital milometer. I never had a shed in my back patio, so I had to keep it safe in my lounge. I got fed up with avoiding all the very bad potholes in my neighbourhood and the bike, with its large battery, was too heavy for me. So as I did not feel safe on this marvellous bike this went to Cash Converters as well. They know me there, as I have sold them a lot of very good merchandise over the years.

My first psychiatrist in Southampton was Professor Chris Nunn, who was very understanding. I was with him for a few years in the mid 1980's till about 1995. He had been Margaret's doctor as well. He retired to Thurso and spent time fishing off his yacht with his new wife, so I was told by a nurse.

Since 1999 my bipolar illness has been taken care of by Dr Steve Brown, who kindly wrote the introduction to this book, and I would like to thank him from the bottom of my heart for the guidance he has given me in writing it. He is a great thinking man who deliberates for a while before speaking his well-prepared thoughts. He has seen me in all my different moods, both in and out of hospital, mainly as an outpatient at Cannon House in Shirley, Southampton. I understand that he plays the saxophone well in a group called 'Kenwood and the Mixers' and that he is known as 'Wayne Fury' in them.

Dr Brown took me off of lithium carbonate after thirty years on it, because blood tests showed that it had affected my kidney function. They are now working at about fifty per cent and my main mood leveller has been changed to sodium valproate. I also take Trazadone, Procyclidine and Citalopram, as well as a few others for high cholesterol, high blood pressure, angina, and diabetes type two. This concoction keeps me quite well most of the time, but I still get the lows and highs at various intervals. But I seem to stay pretty normal for about three months at a time.

Also I would like to thank my brilliant dentist and dear friend Miltiadis Papamichail, known to me as Miltos. He kindly wrote the poetic foreword for this book. He has helped me in the past when I have been down and laughed at my jokes when I've been high. We are always pleased to see each other and it was Miltos who encouraged me to write this autobiography as he said it would be cathartic for me. Indeed I can now say that it has been very liberating and cleansing. Thanks again, Miltos.

I must also thank John Burns from the Baptist Church. He has visited me every other Tuesday evening come rain or shine for many years now. He always has something cheery to say and tells me about his outings as he likes walking in the countryside with his wife Sara. We sometimes go for a walk on the common during the summer months and he takes me out in his car for a meal occasionally. Sometimes he needs help with a couple of clues from his Sunday newspaper and I am always able to oblige with my vast amount of books. He is always there at the end of the phone to assist me with any problems I might have or just to pop round for a chat.

I have been going to Morris House now for a year and it definitely makes me feel better to know that there is something to get up for in the mornings and somewhere to go and talk to kindred spirits. The actual house has closed down now, but Kevin Thomas, our manager, worked diligently to get us into two other new venues, the Central Hall and the Central Baptist Church. Dave is the very pleasant vicar at the latter and every Friday he bakes jacket potatoes for us with beans and/or cheese for just £1.75p. As Kevin said himself, "It's not the building that makes the club but the people in it". So now we are known as "The Friends of Morris House". We used to have meals cooked for us every weekday at the house and they were done on a shoestring budget and only cost £1.50 a day and drinks all day were 50p, so that was just £2 per day all in! They were cooked by four lovely ladies taking turns in the sometimes very hot kitchen. I'd like to thank Annie, Jane, Sandy and Sally - the latter has just become a mum.

I remember once Annie took me and my friend Benny out in her car to Farley Mount, where we had a nice stroll up to the summit and looked down on a beautiful panoramic view all around. Then she drove us on to East Wellow, where we parked up at the Church of St Margaret and viewed Florence Nightingale's grave with the humble inscription 'F.N. Born 12 May 1820 Died 13 August 1910' on her obelisk. As chance would have it there was a funeral going on as we were there and the service was relayed over some loudspeakers in the doorway where the undertakers were standing.

Then to cheer us all up we went to Carlos' Ice Cream Parlour nearby at Wellow, where we had a delicious ice cream and spoke to the owners. Then we looked at the pigs and chickens in the garden. We just got back in the nick of time to have our dinners.

At the new club we have a lovely Asian lady called Sam who looks after us. As I write she is leaving us, but there is a possibility that she may be coming back. We all hope so.

Kevin is leaving too after many good years as a competent and friendly manager.

I believe Brendan O'Reilly will be our new manager. He is a good man from Donegal in Eire. He used to work at the Maudsley Hospital, Denmark Hill in London, with Jo Brand the comedienne, who was the shop steward there.

Epilogue

Overall it's been a pretty happy life, and I'm thankful for the lovely family I've had and all the good times we've had together. Although I could have thrived more without the traumas and depressions, there have always been very good people around for me, especially the mental health folks, who have helped to lift the blues from my mind. They have even put up with my agitated highs as well. I must also thank all the GPs I've had, especially Dr Henry Dean, who I see now, and some of his colleagues.

No doubt I will have my low periods again but I "hang on in there". They usually disappear within a fortnight and normality returns once again, so I can live a near normal life.

I must lastly thank my sister, Ann Maria, for all the love and deep understanding she has shown to me over the many, many years of my wonderful life.